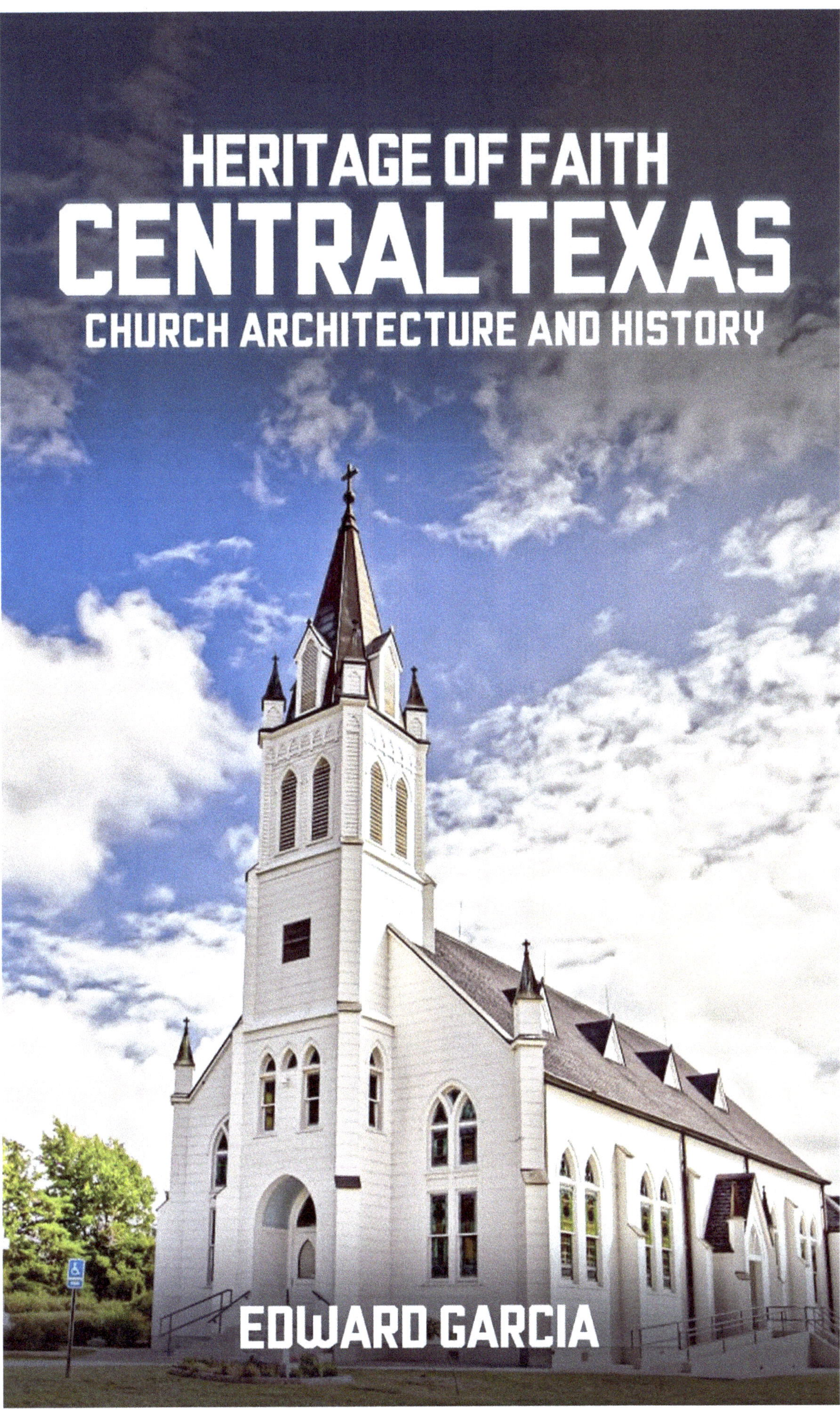

HERITAGE OF FAITH
CENTRAL TEXAS
CHURCH ARCHITECTURE AND HISTORY
EDWARD GARCIA

"Heritage of Faith: Central Texas Church Architecture and History"

By
Edward Garcia

INTRODUCTION

Beginning as early as the year 293, churches have established themselves as landmarks and guiding lights to millions. Whether you grew up attending church every Sunday with your family, dressed to the nines and on your best behavior, or saw them televised in your favorite movie, or perhaps during an influential leader's wedding, funeral, or coronation, the undeniable importance of the church is evident in the various ceremonies that have taken place through not only our own eyes but also the eyes of our ancestors. For centuries, these weddings, funerals, and coronations have often been set in extraordinary cathedrals—hundreds of years old and preserving the spiritual godliness sought by many diverse and devout believers.

Typically, when one thinks of these gracefully stunning and heavenly churches, their minds tend to wander to the glorious Saint Peter's Basilica in Rome, the captivating Cathedral of Santa Maria del Fiore in Florence, Italy, or the spectacular Holy Resurrection Cathedral in Chiyoda-ku, Tokyo. But if you looked a little closer, you'd see that some of the most beautiful churches can be found a lot closer to home.

If you were to take a peaceful drive throughout the Texas countryside, you would be surprised just how many magnificent and astonishing churches are sitting right in your own backyard, while others can be found concealed among superstructures within our cities. All you have to do is step outside and seek them; wait as they come to you and gaze in awe.

The idea for this book first began several years ago. I found myself often driving from South Texas to North Texas, sometimes making several trips a month. It wasn't long before I learned that driving on the backroads was a much easier and safer route than the interstate highways. At least this kept me away from the constant traffic jams that never seemed to end and the numerous construction zones that could sometimes turn a very peaceful drive into a monotonous one very fast.

It was during one of these monthly trips when a good friend of mine, Justin Wied, sent me a link to some of the painted churches in Central Texas, which just so happened to be along my route. He suggested that it might be a good idea to stop at one of these churches every now and then during my travels, as they could make for an interesting exploration break.

As someone who has always had an interest in history, I knew I would be fascinated to learn about the old churches Justin had brought to my attention. However, I wasn't aware of just how much I would fall in love with not only the beauty of the churches but also the history that lay within them.

From the moment I stepped into that first church, I was stunned by the beauty and intricate history that had led to them still standing in that very moment. I soon became even more intrigued, especially with discovering old, historic, or just spiritually inspiring churches within the state. Thus, my journey began, but not even I was prepared to learn about just how many of these heavenly buildings rested amongst us. Some were even hidden, but the stories from the past they divulged quickly became some of the most beautiful history I had ever heard, making me fall even more in love with the structures themselves.

This book contains photographs of some of the most incredible churches I have had the pleasure of visiting, and hopefully, they are able to give you an insight into the identity of the Christian communities that helped build these breathtaking religious structures.

ACKNOWLEDGEMENTS

The pleasure of discovering and having the ability to visit these amazing churches has been the reward of a lifetime. Words cannot convey how it feels stepping into one of these spectacular structures and experiencing that feeling of sanctity; it's indescribable.

All the time, travel, and research to discover and pinpoint these beautiful churches could not be possible without the support of my close family and friends. A heartfelt thank you goes to my wife, Anna Lisa Garcia, for allowing me to pursue my newfound passion. My daughter, Arianna Garcia, for reading and correcting early drafts, and Trevor Holster, for reviewing later drafts. My brother, Hector Garcia, for scouting out some of these inspiring churches, and Scott Rasbury for keeping me company during some of these trips. Of course, none of this could be possible without Justin Wied introducing me to the painted churches in Central Texas, which ignited my passion for awe-inspiring places of worship. A big thank you to Beth Satterwhite Williamson for encouraging me to write this book, and Clark Jones with Amazon Publishing for putting it all together.

I especially want to thank all the people who built, preserved, and told the remarkable stories surrounding these magnificent buildings, and above all I want to give thanks to The Lord our God for giving me the ability to do this.

CENTRAL TEXAS CHURCHES

SAINT MARY'S CATHOLIC CHURCH - HIGH HILL, TEXAS (PAINTED CHURCH)

Saint Mary's Catholic Church, also known as Nativity of Mary Blessed Virgin Catholic Church, is located in High Hill, Texas, on Farm to Market Road 2672, just northwest of Schulenburg, Texas.

In the 1860s, German and Austrian Catholic immigrants settled in the area, and in 1861, the first mass was celebrated in a private home in High Hill by Father Gury. In 1869, the original Saint Mary's Church was built, but it was quickly outgrown as the community continued to prosper. A larger church was built in 1876, with the original church being repurposed as a school for the community. Local parishioners donated stained-glass windows for the second church.

As the community continued to grow, it became evident that an even larger church was needed to accommodate the parishioners. The third and current church was built in 1906, with the windows from the second church installed in the new structure.

Saint Mary's is a red brick building of Gothic Revival design. Inside, the Stations of the Cross were imported from Italy, and the interior is beautifully painted with an amazing altar. Saint Mary's is known as the Queen of the Painted Churches.

Church was designed by Texas church architect Leo M.J. Dielmann

Builder Frank Bohlmann of Schulenburg, Texas, with help from parishioners.

The interior of the church was painted by German artists Ferdinand Stockert and Hermann Kern in 1912.

Stockert and Kern painted designs on canvas and affixed them to the church's wooden walls, resembling wallpaper

The alters were handmade by a company called The Smith Brothers near San Antonio, Texas.

Statue of The Sacred Heart of Jesus with open arms.

Remarkable alter with comprehensive detail.

The central altar was made in two pieces and contains a stained-glass crucifix with the Blessed Mother on top, Saint Peter and Saint Paul to the left and right of the crucifix, and angels surrounding it.

The alters are of German/Czech cultural heritage design.

Side altars are of Blessed Mother Mary holding Baby Jesus and Saint Joseph

Beautiful side-alters on the top right and bottom left photographs.

Statues were shipped from Germany.

The support columns are made of marbleized wood, which gives them the appearance of marble

Each support column has a statue of a Saint

The pews were intentionally made at an uncomfortable angle so parishioners wouldn't get too comfortable and fall asleep.

Sculpture of Michelangelo's La Pieta, Mother Mary holding Jesus after the crucifixion

18 stained-glass windows, made in Germany, were purchased between 1884 and 1889 and used in the current church.

Saint Michael the Archangel.

SAINT MARY'S CHURCH OF THE ASSUMPTION - PRAHA, TEXAS
(PAINTED CHURCH)

Saint Mary's Church of the Assumption Catholic Church in Praha is located off Farm to Market Road 1295, east of Flatonia, Texas. In 1858, the community originally named Mulberry was renamed Praha by Czech settlers after Prague, Czechoslovakia. The first Saint Mary's Catholic Church, a wooden structure, was built by Czech settlers in 1865 and was the first Roman Catholic Church between San Antonio and Houston.

The current church, the fourth one at the same location, was built in 1895. It is of Gothic Revival style and still preserves its initial appearance.

According to folklore, a keg of beer was offered to the man who would affix the cross at the top of the steeple, which is approximately 130 feet high. A local man took up the challenge, and as we can see, there is a cross there, so I am sure he enjoyed the fruits of his labor!

One of the first things you notice when you walk up to Saint Mary's Church of the Assumption is the large crucifix to the left of the front steps and the beautifully painted front doors. The interior is typical of the painted churches, where immigrant settlers freehandedly stenciled, etched, and painted the walls and ceilings.

The exterior was remodeled in 1930.

Swiss-born artist Gottfried Flury from Moulton, Texas, painted much of the interior.

The name Gottfried means "friend of God."

Flury mixed his own paints and used "secret recipes and unique techniques" for his work.

The exterior is made of hand-cut, locally quarried stone by parishioners, and the inside is made of wood.

The current church was built by Czech settlers in 1895 (Czechs were Slavic people from the provinces of Moravia and Bohemia in what is now Czechoslovakia).

Local artist Gene A. Mikulik (who passed away in 1997), a house painter by trade, would touch up the statues at the church and add gold leafing and new paint to the alters.
Statues and stained-glass windows shipped from Bohemia.

Alter with Jesus at the top, then Jesus with (open arms) Sacred Heart of Jesus at the left and the Virgin Mary at the Right.

Bottom left is a side-alter of Saint Joseph holding the Child Jesus. Alters were made by a company called The Smith Brothers near San Antonio, Texas,

Beautifully painted and etched ceiling with incredible detail.

The Crucifixion and Jesus laying in the tomb.

Angel holding the stoup of holy water at the entrance of the church.

Inside view of the beautifully painted front doors.

THE NINE BOYS OF PRAHA CHAPELS - PRAHA, TEXAS

Three small chapels are located on the grounds of Saint Mary's Church of the Assumption Catholic Church in Praha, Texas. According to placards in the chapels, during World War II, nine men from the small community of Praha were killed in battle. Praha, a community with a population of about one hundred at the time, suffered the highest percentage of casualties during the war – more than any other city in the United States.

The three small stone chapels were constructed in 1945 around the church, each dedicated to three of the Nine Boys of Praha. A small cemetery located behind the church is where the nine soldiers (one empty grave) were laid to rest.

The Nine Boys of Praha are:

PFC. Robert Bohuslav. died March 5, 1943, in North Africa.

PFC. Rudolf Barta. died June 16, 1944, in France.

S/SGT. George Pavlicek. died July 7, 1944, in France.

PFC. Jaromir Vaculik. died July 23, 1944, in France.

PVT. Josef Lev. died July 24, 1944, in New Guinea.

PVT. Edward Sbrusch. died September 7, 1944, at Sea (Empty Grave).

PFC. Edward Marek. died September 26, 1944, in the Western Pacific.

PFC. Adolf Rab. died December 27, 1944, in Italy.

PFC. Anton Kresta, Jr. died February 12, 1945, in the Philippines.

Saint Mary Grotto on the southwest side of the church.

Cemetery behind Saint Mary's Church of the Assumption in Praha. This is where the Nine Boys of Praha are buried.
Lt. Col. Valenta is also honored on the same monument.
Reverend Marcus Valenta, Lt. Col., is buried in the Praha Cemetery.

Three identical small chapels, each chapel honoring three of the Nine Boys of Praha

Chapels constructed from local stone.

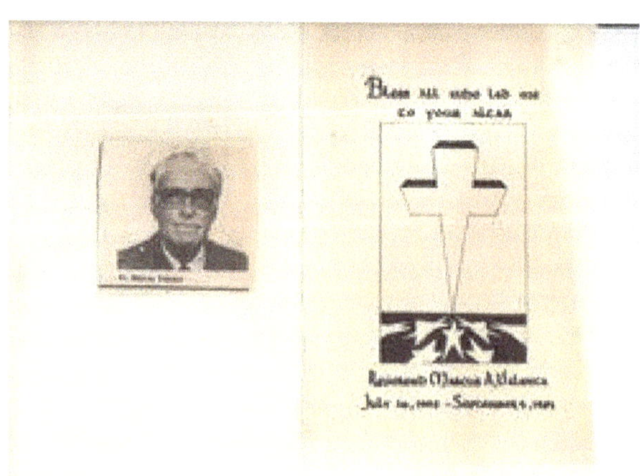

Reverend Marcus Valenta, Lt. Col. U.S. Army Chaplain, a survivor of the Pearl Harbor attack, initiated the building of the three small chapels.

Honoring the nine boys of Praha – their names and photographs
All nine soldiers were members of Saint Mary's Church of the Assumption, and of the church's Men's Choir.

SAINT PAUL'S LUTHERAN CHURCH - SERBIN, TEXAS (PAINTED CHURCH)

Saint Paul's Lutheran Church in Serbin, Texas, was built in 1871 by German immigrants. In the 1850s, German immigrants led by Pastor Johann Kilian settled in what is now Serbin. The immigrants consisted mostly of Wends from the eastern part of Germany. They spoke Wendish, which is closely related to Polish and Czech.

In 1855, a small wooden two-room cabin was built, with one room serving as a home for the pastor and the other as a church and school. The church side was called Saint Peter's Lutheran Church. The community continued to grow, and in 1867, construction began on a larger stone church, which was completed in 1870. Cultural differences had always existed between the two groups, and one issue was which language would be spoken during church services. Eventually, the congregation split, and the German-speaking immigrants decided to build their own church.

The German-speaking immigrants built a stone church in 1871 and named it Saint Paul's Lutheran Church. By 1914, the structure of Saint Peter's had declined, and German was the predominant language spoken in the area. There seemed to be no reason for two separate congregations to exist. Therefore, the two congregations joined as one, worshipping at Saint Paul's Lutheran Church.

Saint Paul's Lutheran Church is the only non-Catholic painted church in the Schulenburg area. The church side of the original wooden cabin used by Pastor Kilian was restored and relocated to the south side of Saint Paul's.

Pastor Kilian lived in a wooden cabin until his death in 1884.

After his death, a portion of the cabin was destroyed, and in 2004, the remaining portion was moved to Saint Paul's Lutheran Church grounds and restored.

The original restored cabin/church used by Pastor Kilian, this is the church side of the building.

The community painted the church.

The pulpit is nearly 20 feet above the lower floor.

The balcony extends around the interior of the church.

The church is a double-decker, an old Christian custom (since about 300 A.D.), women and children sat on the balcony while the men sat at the bottom. Saint Paul's was the opposite, where the men sat on the balcony, and the women and children sat at the bottom.

**Beautiful color combination and
unique marble columns.**

**I love the color of the pipe organ
– so pretty!
E. Pfeifer & Son 1904 Pipe Organ,
still operational.**

Notice how high the pulpit is – it's on the second floor above the alter and said to be the highest pulpit in Texas.

SAINTS CYRIL AND METHODIUS CATHOLIC CHURCH - DUBINA, TEXAS (PAINTED CHURCH)

In 1856, Czech settlers arrived in Dubina, making it the first Czech settlement in Texas. It is estimated that 70 to 90 percent of these immigrants were Catholic, and they built their first church, named St. Joseph's, in 1877. The steeple was topped with an iron cross made by a freed slave and blacksmith, Tom Lee. Unfortunately, in 1909, the church was destroyed by a hurricane.

A new church was built and named Saints Cyril and Methodius Catholic Church. Construction was completed in 1911, and the iron cross from the first church topped the new steeple. In the 1950s, the original interior of the church was thought to be distracting and was painted over with white paint, covering all the astonishing designs, including angels, vines, and oak leaves that had been painted on the walls and ceiling.

Decades later, older parishioners recalled the extraordinarily beautiful interior of the church before it was painted over. In 1983, parishioners, spearheaded by Judge Ed Janecka along with Butch Koenig, launched efforts to restore the interior to its original design. The ceilings are now a beautiful soft blue color with golden stars, and vines and oak leaves are etched along the walls and windows of the church.

Iron Cross made by freed slave and blacksmith, Tom Lee

By Architect Leo Deilmann

After the Hurricane of 1909 destroyed the original church, the community raised $5,571.90 to build a new church.

The community helped with the painting of the church

Vines, Oak Leaves, and angels adorn the blue ceiling and walls

During the renovation in the 1980s, original designs and stencils were uncovered

No records exist on who painted the original interior of the church

Beautiful artwork on the ceiling of the church and a lovely alter with incredible detail. - I love the way the sun is shining on the cross at the right of the alter.

Statues and Alters shipped from Europe

SAINT JOHN THE BAPTIST CATHOLIC CHURCH - AMMONNSVILLE, TEXAS (PAINTED CHURCH)

Saint John the Baptist Catholic Church is located on Farm to Market Road 1383 in Ammannsville, Texas, and is the third church at this location. Ammannsville was founded in 1845 by German and Czech Catholic immigrants. Without their own church, they would attend Mass at nearby Bluff or Dubina. As the community began to grow and prosper, it became apparent that a local church was needed.

The citizens of Ammannsville built the first Saint John the Baptist Church in 1890. Unfortunately, as was true with other churches in the area, the church was destroyed by a hurricane in 1909. In 1910, a new church was built using wood from the old church, but as fate would have it, the second church was destroyed by a fire in 1917.

In 1919, a third church, the current Gothic Revival style church, was built. It is known as the Pink Church because of its rosy-colored interior and beautiful stained-glass windows. The old graveyard, established when the first church was built in the late 1800s, is adjacent to the church.

Architect – John Bujnock

Artist – Fred Donecker and Sons painted the interior

The pale, rosy pink color of the interior

Architect – John Bujnock

Artist – Fred Donecker and Sons painted the interior

The pale, rosy pink color of the interior

Amazingly beautiful alter with Jesus and John the Baptist at the very top.

Alters by J. Henry, Sievers alter was manufactured in San Antonio, Texas, and assembled in Ammonnsville.

Top left – central-alter with Jesus the Shephard on the communion table, the other three photos are of the two side-alters.

The current church was built on the concrete footprint of the second church, which had burned.

The two angel statues holding the holy water at the church entrance were found discarded in the attic of the old rectory and were restored by Gene A. Mikulik.

Painted windows are Tiffany-style.

Local Artist Gene A. Mikulik repainted the statues.

Cemetery from the 1800s on the grounds of the church.

SAINT MARTIN'S CATHOLIC CHURCH – TEXAS HIGHWAY 237 WARRENTON, TEXAS (THE WORLD'S SMALLEST ACTIVE CATHOLIC CHURCH)

In 1888, Saint Martin's Catholic Church was built approximately one mile east of Warrenton and three miles south of Round Top along Texas Highway 237. Saint Martin's was established as a mission of Saint John the Baptist Catholic Church in Fayetteville. By 1915, attendance at the mission church had diminished to a handful, so the mission was disassembled by order of The Bishop and Saint John the Baptist elders to use the wood from the mission to build a church school in Fayetteville.

The parishioners of Warrenton were determined to have their own mission, so they built a tiny church, approximately 192 square feet, at the same location as the original church with surplus wood from the school construction. In 1968, the church school in Fayetteville closed, and the altar, bell, and small statues were transported back to Saint Martin's.

The small wooden church has no electricity, insulation, or modern amenities. There are six small pews on either side of the church, which can seat approximately twenty people. Mass is celebrated once a month for intentions left at the altar by visitors. Saint Martin's still watches over the original cemetery on the church grounds.

Its simplicity is what makes Saint Martin's such an astounding place of worship.

The oldest grave in the cemetery is of Jan Blaha, born in Moravia in 1826 and died in Texas in 1889

So small and simple yet so beautiful in spirit.

Saint Martin's still overlooking the old cemetery.

The church is approximately 192 square feet

Large oil painting of Saint Martin – patron saint of soldiers

HERITAGE OF FAITH
CENTRAL TEXAS
CHURCH ARCHITECTURE AND HISTORY

HISTORIC AND AWE-INSPIRING CHURCHES IN TEXAS IS MOSTLY ABOUT CHURCHES BUILT IN THE 1800'S BY IMMIGRANTS (MOSTLY EUROPEAN) WHO SETTLED IN CENTRAL TEXAS. THE BOOK WILL BRIEFLY INTRODUCE A CHURCH WITH WHERE ITS LOCATED, WHO BUILT IT, WHEN IT WAS BUILT, FOLLOWED BY ANY HISTORICAL DATA ABOUT THE CHURCH. THE INTRODUCTION IS FOLLOWED BY 8 TO 10 PHOTOS OF THE CHURCH. MOST OF THE CHURCHES ARE CALLED PAINTED CHURCHES BECAUSE IMMIGRANTS WHO BUILT THEM WOULD PAINT THE WALLS, CEILINGS AND ARCHES IN COLORFUL PATTERNS TO RESEMBLE CHURCHES IN THEIR HOMELANDS.

www.ingramcontent.com/pod-product-compliance
Lightning Source LLC
Chambersburg PA
CBHW040739150726
48196CB00011B/656